The Big Nursery Rhyme Songbook

"There are perhaps no days of our childhood we
lived so fully as those we spent with a favourite book."

Marcel Proust

Wise Publications
part of The Music Sales Group

London / New York / Paris / Sydney / Copenhagen / Madrid / Tokyo / Berlin

Published by
Wise Publications
14-15 Berners Street, London W1T 3LJ,
United Kingdom.

Exclusive Distributors:
Music Sales Limited
Distribution Centre, Newmarket Road,
Bury St Edmunds, Suffolk IP33 3YB,
United Kingdom.
Music Sales Corporation
257 Park Avenue South, New York, NY 10010,
United States of America.
Music Sales Pty Limited
20 Resolution Drive, Caringbah, NSW 2229,
Australia.

Order No. AM993828
ISBN 978-1-84772-579-0
This book © Copyright 2008 Wise Publications,
a division of Music Sales Limited.

Edited by Ann Barkway.
Illustrated by Rob Hefferan.
Printed in China.
CD recorded, mixed and mastered by
Jonas Persson.
Backing tracks by Rick Cardinali.
Vocals by Bryn Barton, Sara Cowen, Lois Green,
Jean Squires, Zoe Tankard and Natasha Vakil,
led by Debbie Campbell and Ann Barkway.
Stories told by Will Barkway.

Poems...

Stories...

Music...

Baa *Baa* Black *Sheep*

Traditional

Smoothly

Baa baa black sheep, have you a-ny wool? Yes sir,

yes sir, three bags full. One for the mas-ter, one for the

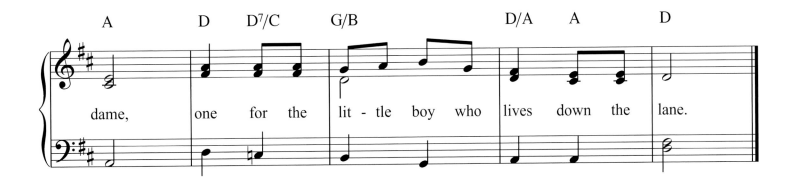

dame, one for the lit-tle boy who lives down the lane.

TRACK 2

The *Barnyard* Song

Traditional

Lively

D   A⁷/E   D/F♯   A⁷/E   D   G

mf 1. I had a cat, and the cat pleased me, I fed my cat un-der

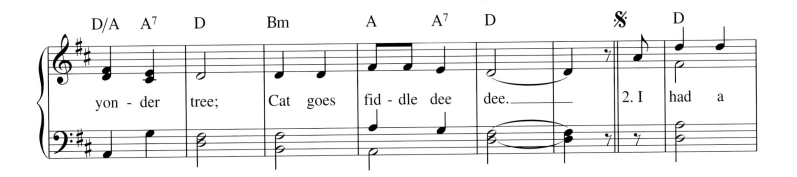

yon - der tree; Cat goes fid - dle dee dee._____ 2. I had a

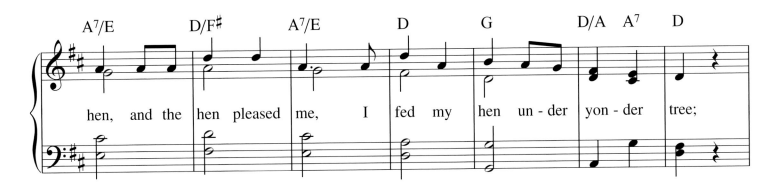

hen, and the hen pleased me, I fed my hen un - der yon - der tree;

(repeat an extra time for each)

Hen goes chim - my chuck, chim - my chuck; Cat goes fid - dle dee dee._____

3   I had a duck…
    …Duck goes quack, quack…

4   I had a pig…
    …Pig goes oink, oink…

5   I had a sheep…
    …Sheep goes baaa, baaa…

6   I had a turkey…
    …Turkey goes gibble-gobble…

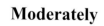

Cock-*A*-Doodle-*Doo*

Traditional

Moderately

Cock - a - doo - dle - doo,   my dame has lost her shoe.   My

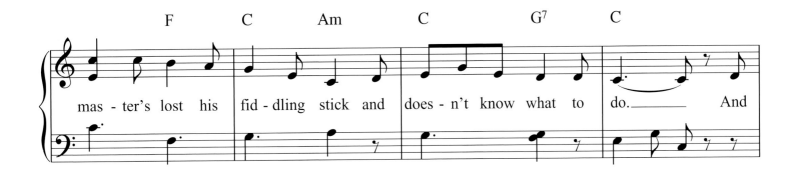

mas - ter's lost his fid - dling stick and does - n't know what to do._____ And

does - n't know what to do,_____ and does - n't know what to do._____ My

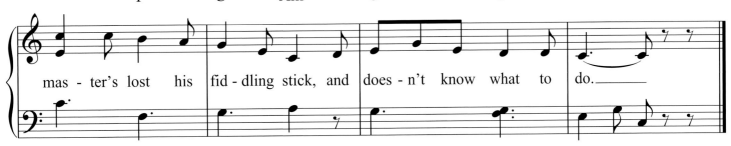

mas - ter's lost his fid - dling stick, and does - n't know what to do._____

Cock-a-doodle-doo, what is my dame to do?
'Til master finds his fiddling stick,
She'll dance without her shoe.

2 She'll dance without her shoe,
She'll dance without her shoe.
'Til master finds his fiddling stick,
She'll dance without her shoe.

Eensy *Weensy* Spider

Traditional

Moderately

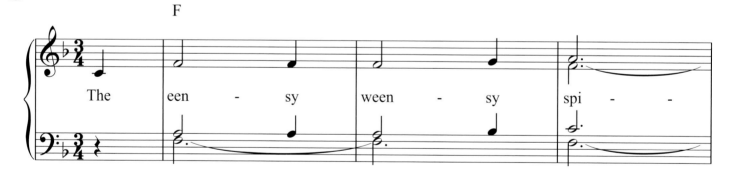

The een - sy ween - sy spi - -

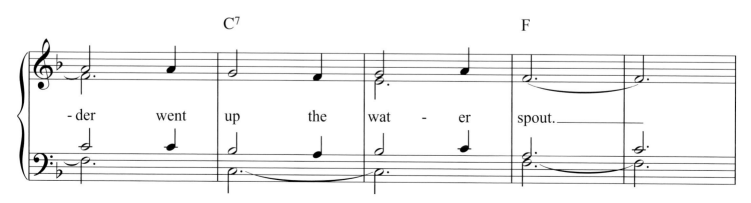

- der went up the wat - er spout. _____

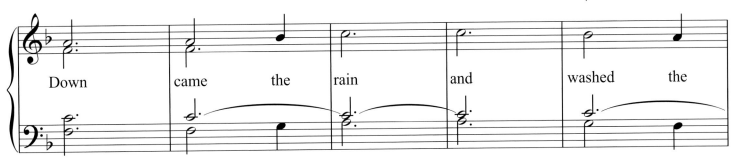

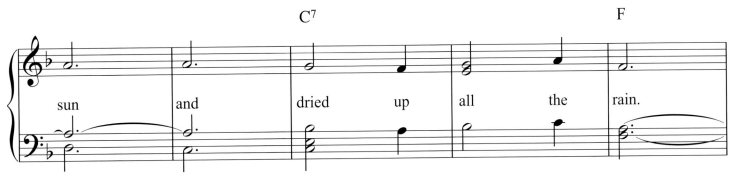

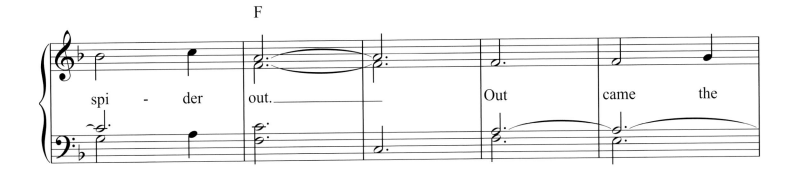

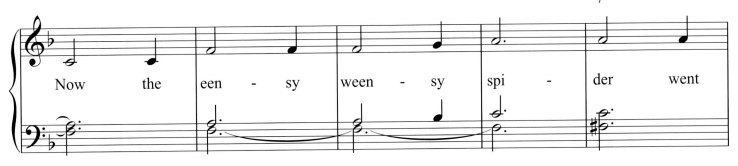

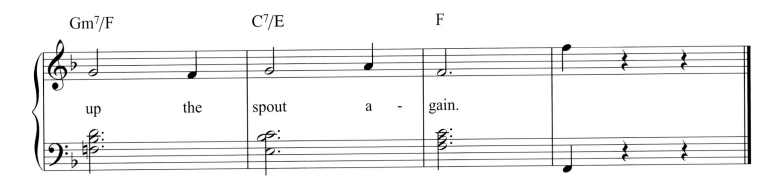

TRACK 5

The *Grand* Old *Duke* Of *York*

Traditional

Brightly

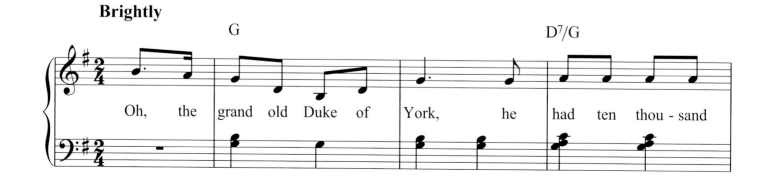

Oh, the grand old Duke of York, he had ten thou - sand

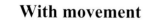

Here *We* Go *Looby* Loo

Traditional

With movement

Here we go loo-by loo, here we go loo-by light,

here we go loo - by loo, all on a Sat - ur - day night.

1. Put your right hand in, put your right hand out,

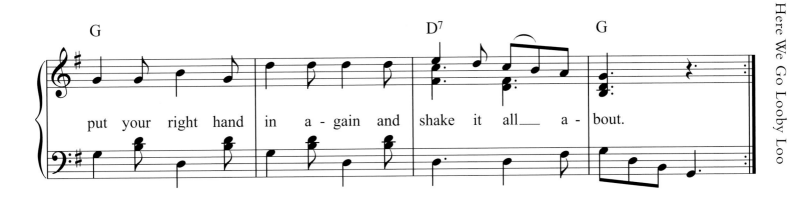

put your right hand in a - gain and shake it all___ a - bout.

Chorus
Here we go looby loo,
Here we go looby light,
Here we go looby loo,
All on a Saturday night.

2 Put your left hand in…

3 Put your right arm in…

4 Put your left arm in…

5 Put your right foot in…

6 Put your left foot in…

7 Put your right leg in…

8 Put your left leg in…

9 Put your back in…

10 Put your front in…

11 Put your head in…

12 Put your whole self in…

Doctor *Foster*

Traditional

Moderately

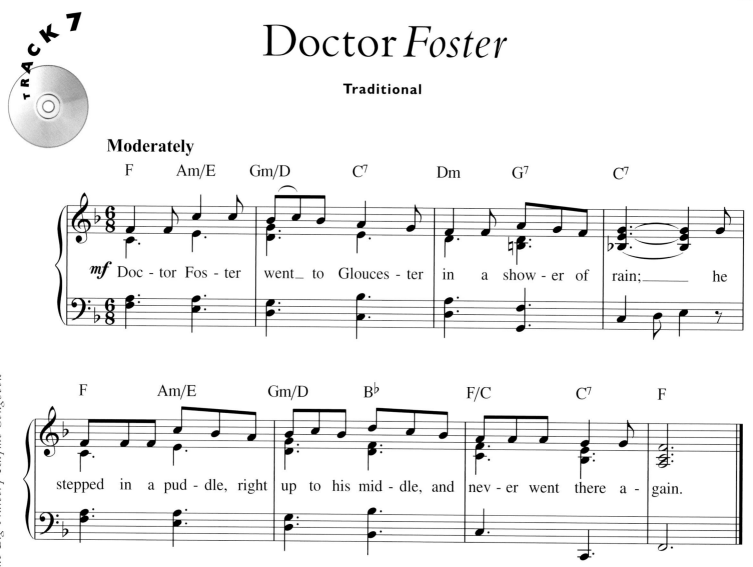

mf Doc - tor Fos - ter | went_ to Glouces - ter | in a show - er of | rain;_____ he

stepped in a pud - dle, right | up to his mid - dle, and | nev - er went there a - | gain.

Goldilocks *And* The *Three* Bears

Traditional

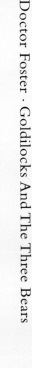

Once upon a time there were Three Bears, who lived together in a house of their own in a wood. One of them was a Little Wee Bear and one was a Middle-Sized Bear and the other was a Great Big Bear. They each had a bowl for their porridge – a little wee bowl for the Little Wee Bear and a middle-sized bowl for the Middle-Sized Bear and a great big bowl for the Great Big Bear; and they each had a chair to sit in – a little wee chair for the Little Wee Bear and a middle-sized chair for the Middle-Sized Bear and a great big chair for the Great Big Bear; and they had each a bed to sleep in – a little wee bed for the Little Wee Bear and a middle-sized bed for the Middle-Sized Bear and a great big bed for the Great Big Bear.

One day, after they had made the porridge for their breakfast, and poured it into their porridge-bowls, they walked out into the wood while the porridge was cooling so that they might not burn their mouths by beginning too soon, for they were polite, well-brought-up Bears. While they were away, a little girl called Goldilocks, who lived at the other side of the wood and had been sent on an errand by her mother, passed by the house, and looked in at the window. Then she peeped in at the keyhole, for she was not at all a well-brought-up little girl. Seeing that there was nobody in the house, she lifted the latch. The door was not fastened, because the Bears were good Bears, who did nobody any harm, and never suspected that anybody would harm them.

So Goldilocks opened the door and went in; and well pleased was she when she saw the porridge on the table. If she had been a well-brought-up little girl she would have waited till the Bears came home, and then, perhaps, they would have asked her to breakfast, for they were good Bears – a little rough or so, as is the manner of Bears, but for all that, very good-natured and hospitable. Goldilocks, however, was an impudent, rude little girl and so she set about helping herself.

First she tasted the porridge of the Great Big Bear, and that was too hot for her. Next she tasted the porridge of the Middle-Sized Bear, but that was too cold for her. Then she went to the porridge of the Little Wee Bear and tasted it, and that was neither too hot nor too cold, but just right. She liked it so well that she ate it all up, every last bit!

Then Goldilocks, who was tired, for she had been catching butterflies instead of running on her errand, sat down in the chair of the Great Big Bear, but that was too hard for her. Then she sat down in the chair of the Middle-Sized Bear, and that was too soft for her, but when she sat down in the chair of the Little Wee Bear, that was neither too hard, nor too soft, but just right. So she seated herself in it, and there she sat till the bottom of the chair came out and down she came, plump upon the ground. That made her very cross, for she was a bad-tempered little girl too.

Now, being determined to rest, Goldilocks went upstairs into the bed-chamber in which the Three Bears slept. First she lay down upon the bed of the Great Big Bear, but that was too high at the head for her. Next she lay down upon the bed of the Middle-Sized Bear, and that was too high at the foot for her. Then she lay down upon the bed of the Little Wee Bear, and that was neither too high at the head, nor at the foot, but just right. So she covered herself up comfortably, and lay there till she fell fast asleep.

By this time the Three Bears thought their porridge would be cool enough for them to eat it properly, so they came home to breakfast. Now careless Goldilocks had left the spoon of the Great Big Bear standing in his porridge.

"Somebody has been at my porridge!" said the Great Big Bear in his great, rough, gruff voice.

Then the Middle-Sized Bear looked at his porridge and saw the spoon was standing in it too.

"Somebody has been at my porridge!" said the Middle-Sized Bear in his middle-sized voice.

Then the Little Wee Bear looked at his, and there was the spoon in the porridge-bowl, but the porridge was all gone!

"Somebody has been at my porridge, and has eaten it all up!" said the Little Wee Bear in his little wee voice.

Upon this, the Three Bears, seeing that someone had entered their house and eaten up the Little Wee Bear's breakfast, began to look about them.

Now the careless Goldilocks had not put the hard cushion straight when she rose from the chair of the Great Big Bear.

"Somebody has been sitting in my chair!" said the Great Big Bear in his great, rough, gruff voice.

The careless Goldilocks had also squatted down the soft cushion of the Middle-Sized Bear.

"Somebody has been sitting in my chair!" said the Middle-Sized Bear in his middle-sized voice.

"Somebody has been sitting in my chair, and has sat the bottom through!" said the Little Wee Bear in his little wee voice.

Then the Three Bears thought they had better make further search in case it was a burglar, so they went upstairs into their bedchamber.

Now careless Goldilocks had pulled the pillow of the Great Big Bear out of its place.

"Somebody has been lying in my bed!" said the Great Big Bear in his great, rough, gruff voice.

And Goldilocks had pulled the bolster of the Middle-Sized Bear out of its place.

"Somebody has been lying in my bed!" said the Middle-Sized Bear in his middle-sized voice.

But when the Little Wee Bear came to look at his bed, there was the bolster in its place, and the pillow was in its place upon the bolster, and upon the pillow…? There was Goldilocks' yellow head – which was not in its place, for she had no business there!

"Somebody has been lying in my bed – and here she is still!" said the Little Wee Bear in his little wee voice.

Now Goldilocks had heard in her sleep the great, rough, gruff voice of the Great Big Bear, but she was so fast asleep that it was no more to her than the roaring of wind, or the rumbling of thunder. She had also heard the middle-sized voice of the Middle-Sized Bear, but it was only as if she had heard someone speaking in a dream. But when she heard the little wee voice of the Little Wee Bear, it was so sharp, and so shrill, that it awakened her at once.

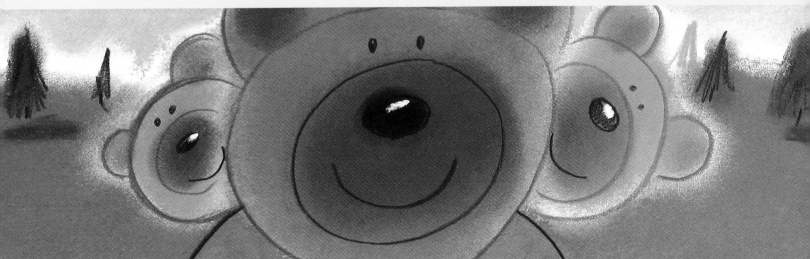

Up she started, and when she saw the Three Bears on one side of the bed, she tumbled herself out at the other, and ran to the window. Now the window was open, because the Bears, like good, tidy Bears as they were, always opened their bedchamber window when they got up in the morning. So naughty, frightened little Goldilocks jumped and whether she broke her neck in the fall, or ran into the wood and was lost there, or found her way out of the wood and got whipped for being a bad girl and playing truant, no one can say, but the Three Bears never saw anything more of her again.

If you see a fairy ring
    In a field of grass,
Very lightly step around,
    Tip-toe as you pass;
Last night fairies frolicked there,
And they're sleeping somewhere near.

If You See A Fairy Ring

Anon

If you see a tiny fay
    Lying fast asleep,
Shut your eyes and rub away,
    Do not stay to peep;
And be sure you never tell,
Or you'll break a fairy spell.

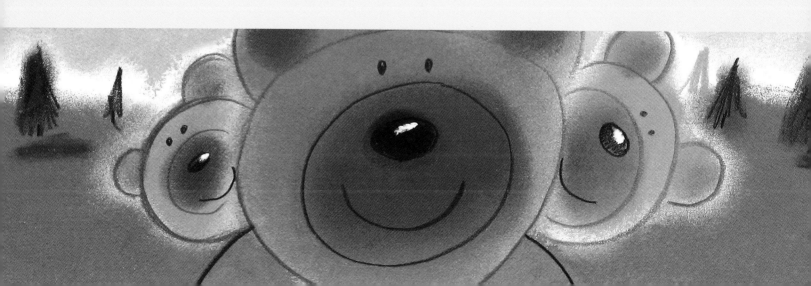

Hickory *Dickory* Dock

Traditional

Fairly bright

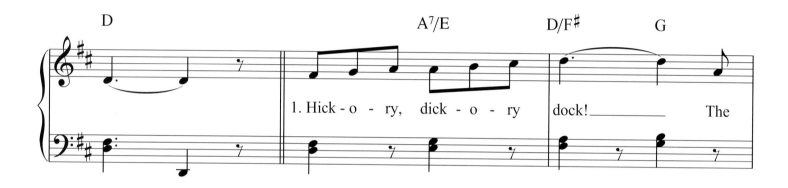

1. Hick - o - ry, dick - o - ry dock!_____ The

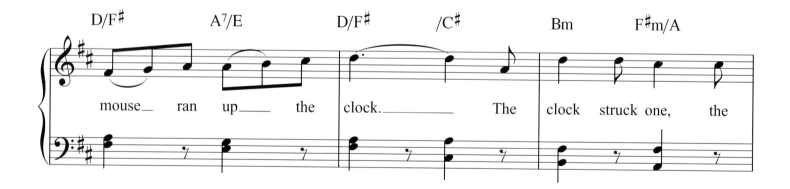

mouse_ ran up___ the clock._____ The clock struck one, the

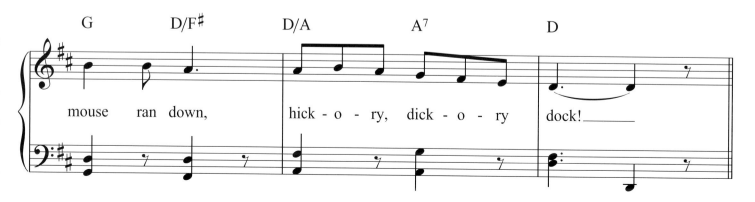

mouse ran down, hick - o - ry, dick - o - ry dock!_____

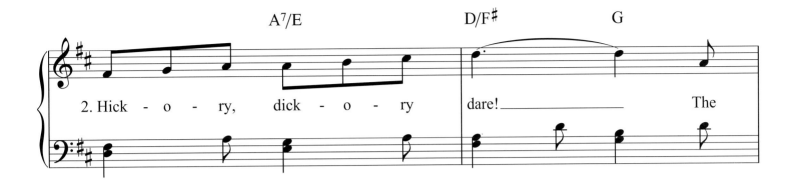

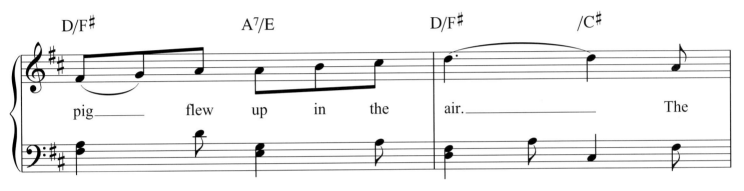

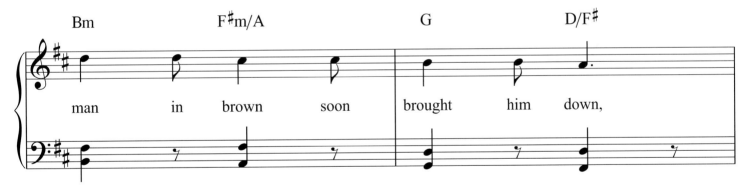

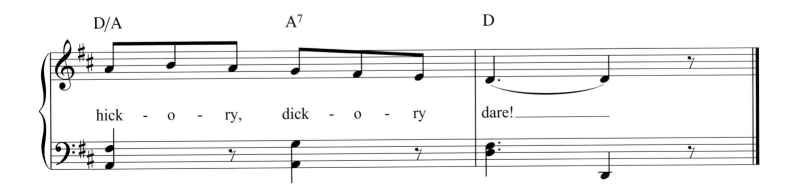

TRACK 11

Here *We* Go 'Round The *Mulberry* Bush

Traditional

With movement

Here we go 'round the mul - b'ry bush, the mul - b'ry

$\text{A}^7/\text{C}^\sharp$ D   G

bush,   the   mul - b'ry   bush.   Here   we   go   'round   the

Em   C D^7 G

mul - b'ry   bush   on   a   cold   and   fros - ty   morn - ing.

2   This is the way we wash our hands…

3   This is the way we wash our clothes…

4   This is the way we dry our clothes…

5   This is the way we iron our clothes…

6   This is the way we sweep the floor…

7   This is the way we brush our hair…

8   This is the way we go to school…

9   This is the way we come back from school…

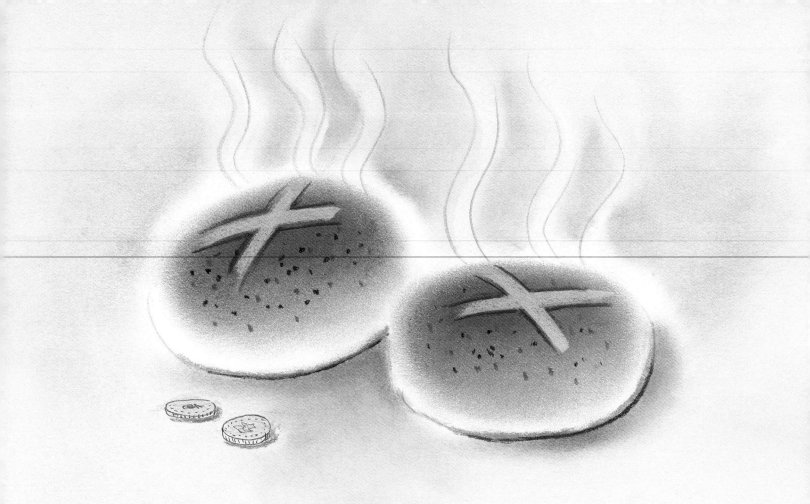

Hot Cross Buns

Traditional

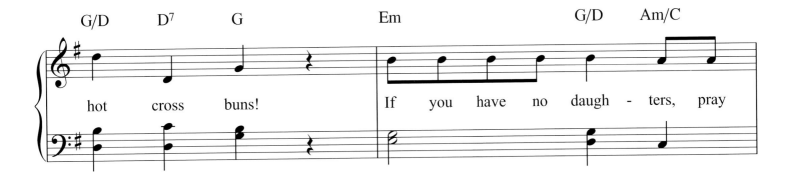

hot   cross   buns!   If   you   have   no   daugh - ters,   pray

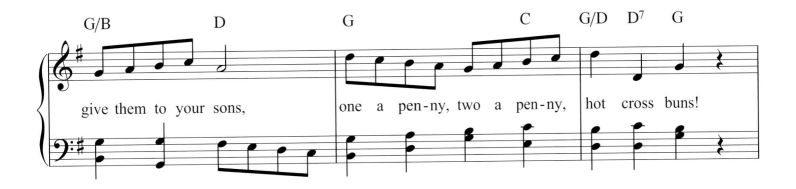

give them to your sons,   one a pen - ny, two a pen - ny, hot cross buns!

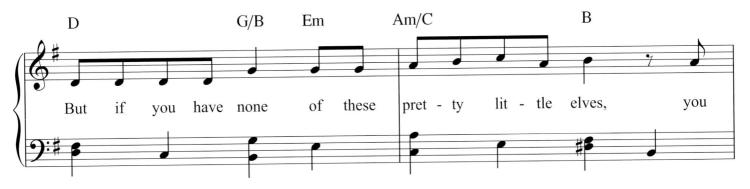

But   if   you   have none   of   these   pret - ty   lit - tle   elves,   you

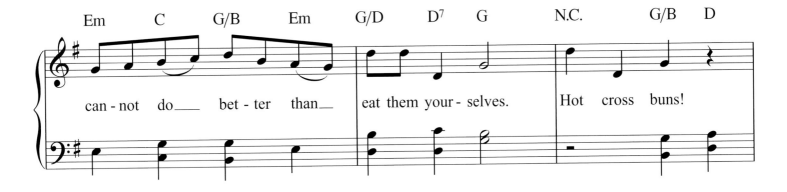

can - not do___ bet - ter than___ eat them your - selves.   Hot   cross   buns!

Hot   cross   buns!   One a pen - ny, two a pen - ny,   hot   cross   buns!

Humpty *Dumpty*

Traditional

The Big Nursery Rhyme Songbook

TRACK 13

Jack *And* Jill

Traditional

Moderately

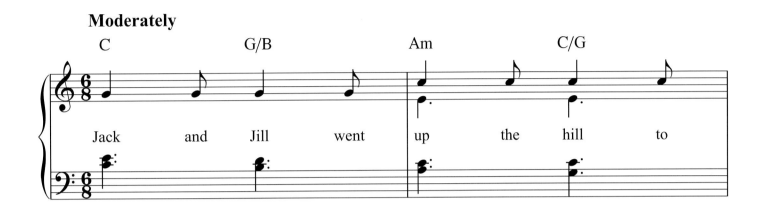

Jack and Jill went up the hill to

fetch a pail of wat - er. Jack fell down and

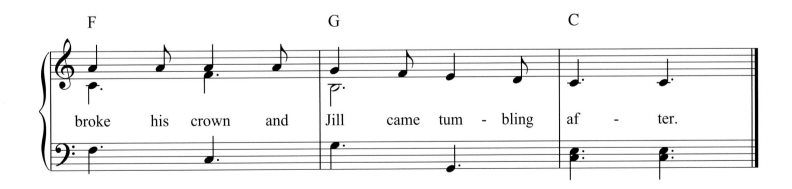

broke his crown and Jill came tum - bling af - ter.

TRACK 15

Little *Bo*-Peep

Traditional

Smoothly

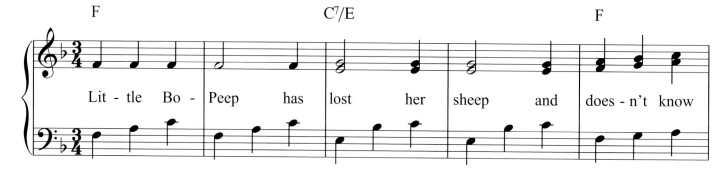

Lit - tle Bo - Peep has lost her sheep and does - n't know

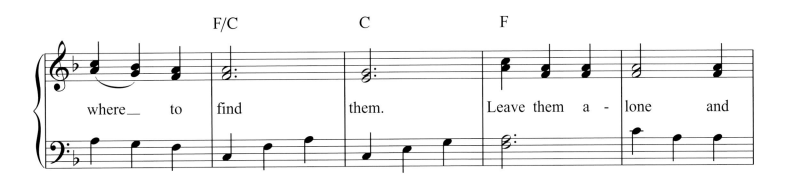

where— to find them. Leave them a - lone and

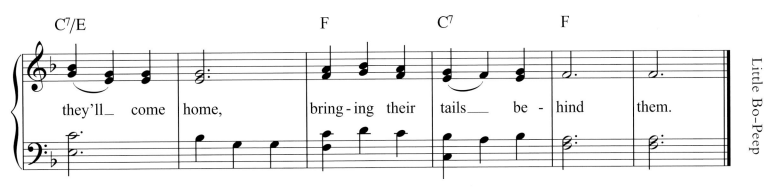

they'll— come home, bring-ing their tails— be - hind them.

2   Little Bo-Peep fell fast asleep,
And dreamed she heard them bleating,
But when she awoke, she found it a joke,
For they were still a-fleeting.

3   Then up she took her little crook,
Determined for to find them,
She found them indeed, but it made her heart bleed,
For they'd left their tails behind them.

Little Bo-Peep

Jack *Be* Nimble

Traditional

Moderately

| F | F/A | Gm | F | Csus⁴ | C | F | F/A | Gm | F | C⁷ |

Jack_ be nim - ble | Jack be quick. | Jack_ jump ov - er the | can - dle_ stick.

| C⁷/E | F | Dm | C⁷ | F | C⁷ | F |

Jack jumped high and | Jack jumped_ low. | Jack jumped ov - er and | burnt his toe.

The *Emperor's* New *Clothes* by *Hans* Christian *Andersen*

Many years ago there lived an emperor, who cared so enormously for beautiful new clothes that he spent all his money upon them. He did not care about his soldiers, nor about the theatre, nor about driving in the park except to show his new clothes. He had a coat for every hour of the day, and just as they say of a king, "He is in council," one always said of him, "The emperor is in the wardrobe."

In the great city in which he lived, it was always very merry – every day a number of strangers arrived there. One day two cheats came; they gave themselves out as weavers, and declared that they could weave the finest stuff anyone could imagine. Not only were their colours and patterns, they said, uncommonly beautiful, but the clothes made of this particular stuff possessed the wonderful quality that they became invisible to anyone who was unfit for the office he held, or was incorrigibly stupid.

"Those would be capital clothes!" thought the emperor. "If I wore those, I should be able to find out what men in my empire are not fit for the places they have; I could distinguish the clever from the stupid. Yes, have the stuff woven for me directly!" And he gave the two cheats a great deal of cash in hand, that they might begin their work at once.

As for them, they put up two looms, and pretended to be working, but they had nothing at all on their looms. They at once demanded the finest silk and the costliest gold; this they put into their own pockets, and worked empty looms till late into the night.

"I should like to know how far they have got on with the stuff," thought the emperor, but he felt quite uncomfortable when he thought that those who were not fit for their offices could not see it. He believed, indeed, that he had nothing to fear for himself, but yet he preferred first to send someone else to see how matters stood. All the people in the whole city knew what peculiar power the stuff possessed, and all were anxious to see how bad or how stupid their neighbours were.

"I will send my honest old minister to the weavers," thought the emperor. "He can judge best how the stuff looks, for he has sense, and no one discharges his office better than he."

35

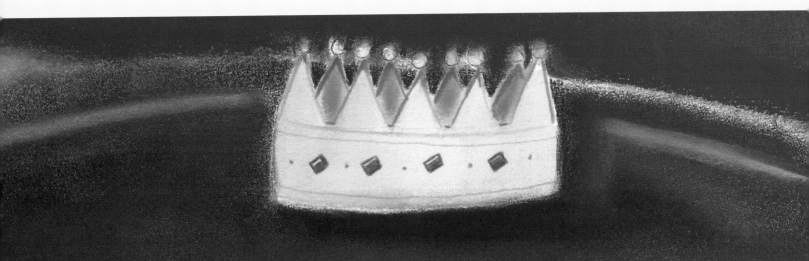

Now the good old minister went out into the hall where the two cheats sat working at the empty looms.

"Mercy preserve us!" thought the old minister, and he opened his eyes wide. "I cannot see anything at all!" But he did not say this.

Both the cheats begged him to be kind enough to come nearer, and asked if he did not approve of the colours and the pattern. Then they pointed to the empty loom, and the poor old minister went on opening his eyes, but he could see nothing, for there was nothing for him to see.

"Mercy!" thought he, "Can I indeed be so stupid? I never thought that, and not a soul must know it. Am I not fit for my office? No, it will never do for me to tell that I could not see the stuff."

"Do you say nothing to it?" said one of the weavers.

"Oh, it is charming – quite enchanting!" answered the old minister, as he peered through his spectacles. "What a fine pattern, and what colours! Yes, I shall tell the emperor that I am very much pleased with it."

"Well, we are glad of that," said both the weavers, and then they named the colours, and explained the strange pattern. The old minister listened attentively, that he might be able to repeat it when he went back to the emperor, and he did so.

Now the cheats asked for more money, and more silk and gold which they declared they wanted for weaving. They put it all into their own pockets and not a thread was put upon the loom, but they continued to work at the empty frames as before.

The emperor soon sent again, dispatching another honest statesman to see how the weaving was going on and if the stuff would soon be ready. He fared just like the first. He looked and looked, but, as there was nothing to be seen but the empty looms, he could see nothing.

"Is not that a pretty piece of stuff?" asked the two cheats, and they displayed and explained the handsome pattern which was not there at all.

"I am not stupid!" thought the man. "It must be my good office, for which I am not fit. It is funny enough, but I must not let it be noticed." And so he praised the stuff which he did not see, and expressed his pleasure at the beautiful colours and the charming pattern.

"Yes, it is enchanting," he said to the emperor.

All the people in the town were talking of the gorgeous stuff. The emperor wished to see it himself while it was still upon the loom. With a whole crowd of chosen men, among whom were also the two honest statesmen who had already been there, he went to the two cunning cheats, who were now weaving with might and main without fibre or thread.

"Is that not splendid?" said the two old statesmen, who had already been there once.

"Does not your majesty remark the pattern and the colours?" And then they pointed to the empty loom, for they thought that the others could see the stuff.

"What's this?" thought the emperor. "I can see nothing at all! That is terrible. Am I stupid? Am I not fit to be emperor? That would be the most dreadful thing that could happen to me."

"Oh, it is *very* pretty!" he said aloud. "It has our exalted approbation." And he nodded in a contented way, and gazed at the empty loom, for he would not say that he saw nothing.

The whole suite whom he had with him looked and looked and saw nothing, any more than the rest, but, like the emperor, they said, "That is pretty!" and counselled him to wear these splendid new clothes for the first time at the great procession that was presently to take place.

"It is splendid, tasteful, excellent!" went from mouth to mouth. On all sides there seemed to be general rejoicing and the emperor gave each of the cheats a cross to hang at his button-hole and the title of Imperial Court Weaver.

The whole night before the morning on which the procession was to take place, the cheats were up, and had lighted more than sixteen candles. The people could see that they were hard at work, completing the emperor's new clothes. They pretended to take the stuff down from the loom; they made cuts in the air with great scissors; they sewed with needles without thread; and at last they said, "Now the clothes are ready!"

The emperor came himself with his noblest cavaliers, and the two cheats lifted up one arm as if they were holding something and said, "See, here are the trousers! Here is the coat! Here is the cloak!" and so on.

"It is as light as a spider's web; one would think one had nothing on, but that is just the beauty of it."

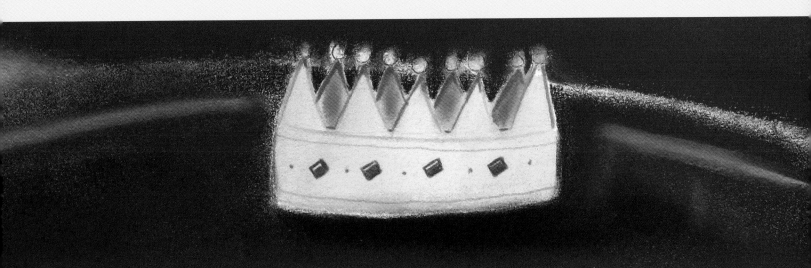

"Yes," said all the cavaliers, but they could not see anything, for nothing was there.

"Does your imperial majesty please to condescend to undress?" said the cheats, "Then we will put the new clothes on you here in front of the great mirror."

The emperor took off his clothes, and the cheats pretended to put on him each of the new garments. They took him round the waist, and seemed to fasten on something, (that was the train), and the emperor turned round and round before the mirror.

"Oh, how well they look! How capitally they fit!" said all. "What a pattern! What colours! That is a splendid dress!"

"They are standing outside with the canopy which is to be borne above your majesty in the procession!" announced the head master of the ceremonies.

"Well, I am ready," replied the emperor. "Does it not suit me well?" And then he turned again to the mirror, for he wanted it to appear as if he contemplated his adornment with great interest.

The chamberlains, who were to carry the train, stooped down with their hands towards the floor, just as if they were picking up the mantle. Then they pretended to be holding something up in the air. They did not dare to let it be noticed that they saw nothing.

So the emperor went in procession under the rich canopy, and everyone in the streets said, "How incomparable are the emperor's new clothes! What a train he has to his mantle! How it fits him!"

No one would let it be perceived that he could see nothing, for that would have shown that he was not fit for his office, or was very stupid. No clothes of the emperor's had ever had such a success as these.

"But he *has* nothing on!" a little child cried out at last.

"Just hear what that innocent says!" said the father, and one whispered to another what the child had said.

"There is a little child that says he has nothing on."

"But he has nothing on!" said the whole people at length, and the emperor shivered, for it seemed to him that they were right, but he thought within himself, "I must go through with the procession."

So he carried himself still more proudly, and the chamberlains held on tighter than ever, and carried the train which did not exist at all.

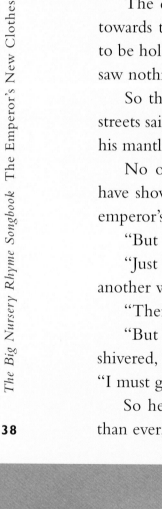

Merrily *We* Roll *Along*

Traditional

Moderately

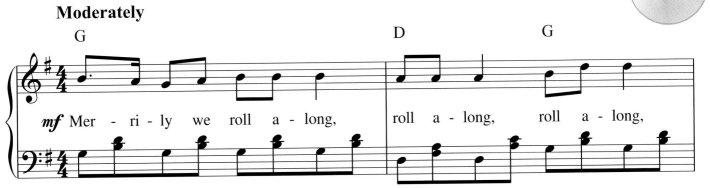

mf Mer - ri - ly we roll a - long, roll a - long, roll a - long,

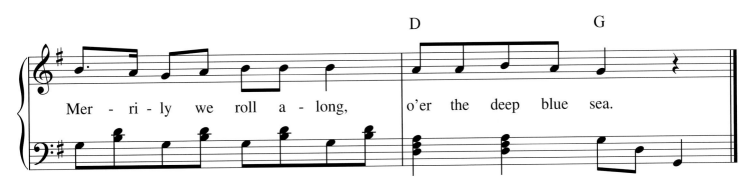

Mer - ri - ly we roll a - long, o'er the deep blue sea.

Merrily We Roll Along

TRACK 19

London *Bridge* Is *Falling* Down

Traditional

With spirit

Lon - don Bridge is | fall - ing down, | fall - ing down, | fall - ing down.

Lon - don Bridge is | fall - ing down, | my fair | la - dy.

The Big Nursery Rhyme Songbook

2 How shall we build it up again?..

3 Build it up with iron bars…

4 Iron bars will bend and break…

5 Build it up with pins and needles…

6 Pins and needles rust and bend…

7 Build it up with penny loaves…

8 Penny loaves will tumble down…

9 Build it up with gold and silver…

10 Gold and silver I've not got…

Michael *Finnegan*

Traditional

Fast

C   C⁷   F

There was an old man called Mi - chael Fin - ne - gan,

There was an old man called Michael Finnegan,
He went fishing with a pin again.
He caught a fish then dropped it in again.
Poor old Michael Finnegan, begin again.

2

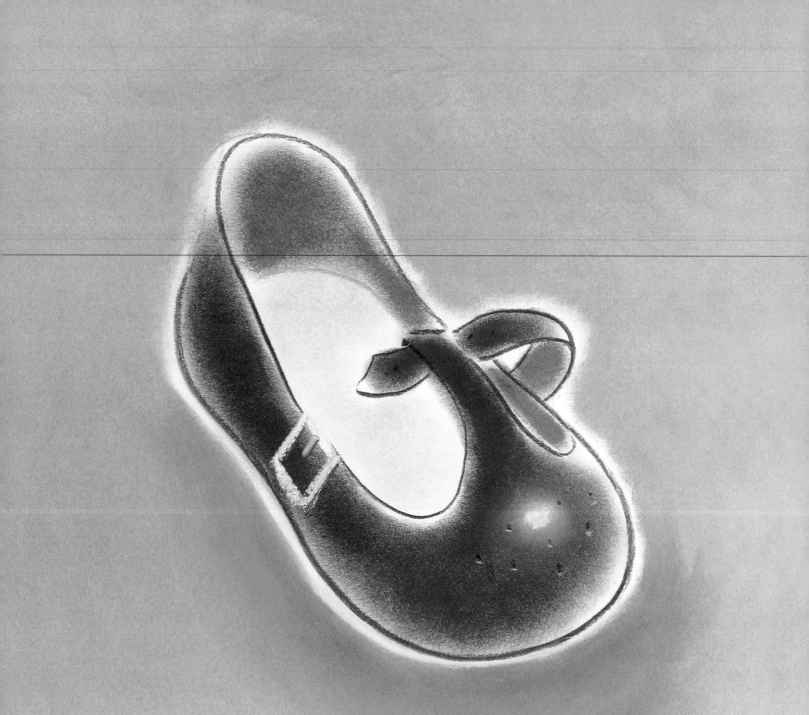

One, *Two*, Buckle *My* Shoe

Traditional

Moderately

C	G⁷	C	G⁷	C	G

One, two, buck - le my shoe, three, four, o - pen the door,

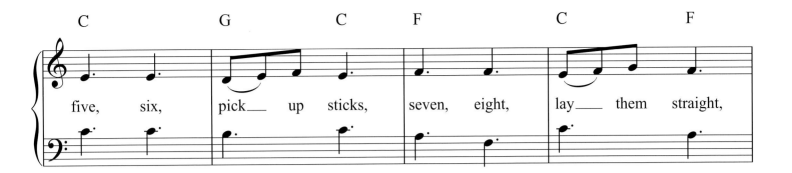

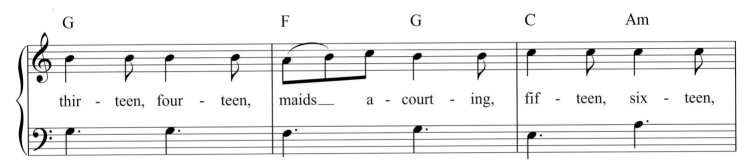

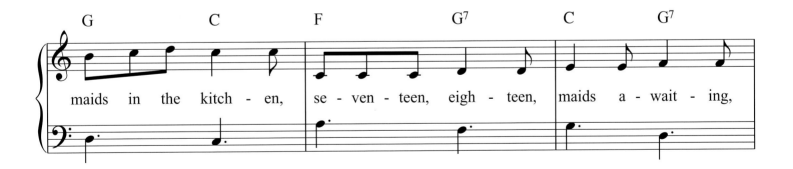

TRACK 22

One *Man* Went *To* Mow

Traditional

Fast

One man went to mow, went to mow a mea-dow.

Repeat as required   **D.C.** **Final bar**

One man and his dog went to mow a mea-dow.

2

Two men went to mow,
Went to mow a meadow.
Two men, one man and his dog
Went to mow a meadow.

3

Three men went to mow,
Went to mow a meadow.
Three men, two men, one man and his dog
Went to mow a meadow.

4   Four men went to mow…

5   Five men went to mow…

6   Six men went to mow…

7   Seven men went mow…

TRACK 23

Oranges *And* Lemons

Traditional

Steadily

G   Am/E   D/F#   G   G/B

"Or - an - ges and | lem - ons," say the | bells of St | Clem- ent's. "You | owe me five

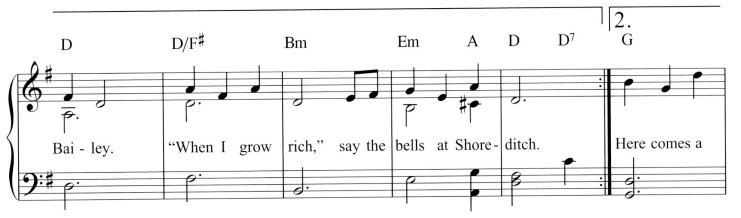

Mary *Had A Little* Lamb

Traditional

Moderately

1. Ma - ry had a
(Verses 3-8 see block lyric)
lit - tle lamb,
lit - tle lamb,

50

lit - tle lamb, Ma - ry had a lit - tle lamb, its

fleece as white as snow. 2. And ev - 'ry - where that

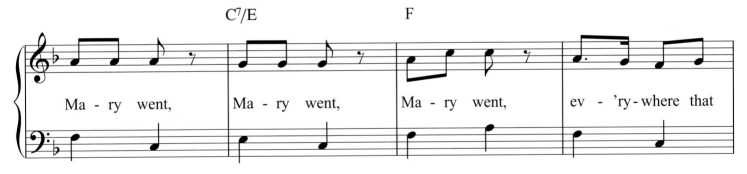

Ma - ry went, Ma - ry went, Ma - ry went, ev - 'ry - where that

Ma - ry went, the lamb was sure to go. 3. It - ply.

3
It followed her to school one day,
School one day, school one day.
It followed her to school one day,
Which was against the rules.

4
It made the children laugh and play,
Laugh and play, laugh and play.
It made the children laugh and play,
To see a lamb at school.

5
And so the teacher turned it out,
Turned it out, turned it out.
And so the teacher turned it out,
But still it lingered near.

6
And waited patiently about,
'Ly about, 'ly about.
And waited patiently about,
'Til Mary did appear.

7
Why does the lamb love Mary so?
Mary so, Mary so?
Why does the lamb love Mary so?
The eager children cry.

8
Why, Mary loves the lamb, you know,
Lamb, you know, lamb, you know.
Why, Mary loves the lamb, you know,
The teacher did reply.

Jack *And* The *Beanstalk*

Traditional
Bonus Story - not included on CD

A long, long time ago, when most of the world was young and folk did what they liked because all things were good, there lived a boy called Jack. His father was bedridden, and his mother, a good soul, was busy early morns and late eves planning and placing how to support her sick husband and her young son by selling the milk and butter which Milky-White, the beautiful cow, gave them without stint. For it was summertime, but winter came on; the herbs of the fields took refuge from the frosts in the warm earth, and though his mother sent Jack to gather what fodder he could get in the hedgerows, he came back as often as not with a very empty sack, for Jack's eyes were so often full of wonder at all the things he saw, that sometimes he forgot to work!

So it came to pass that one morning, Milky-White gave no milk at all – not one drain! The good hard-working mother threw her apron over her head and sobbed, "What shall we do? What shall we do?"

Now, Jack loved his mother. Besides, he felt just a bit sneaky at being such a big boy and doing so little to help, so he said, "Cheer up! Cheer up! I'll go and get work somewhere." And as he spoke, he felt as if he would work his fingers to the bone, but the good woman shook her head mournfully.

"You've tried that before, Jack," she said, "and nobody would keep you. You are quite a good lad but your wits go a-woolgathering. No, we must sell Milky-White and live on the money. It is no use crying over milk that is not here to spill!"

You see, she was a wise as well as a hard-working woman, and Jack's spirits rose.

"Just so," he cried. "We will sell Milky-White and be richer than ever. It's an ill wind that blows no one good. So, as it is market-day, I'll just take her there and we shall see what we shall see."

"But…" began his mother.

"But doesn't butter parsnips," laughed Jack. "Trust me to make a good bargain."

So, as it was washing-day, and her sick husband was more ailing than usual, his mother let Jack set off to sell the cow.

"Not less than ten pounds," she bawled after him as he turned the corner.

Ten pounds, indeed! Jack had made up his mind to twenty! Twenty solid golden sovereigns! He was just settling what he should buy his mother as a fairing out of the money, when he saw a strange little old man on the road who called out, "Good-morning, Jack!"

"Good-morning," replied Jack, with a polite bow, wondering how the strange little old man happened to know his name; though, to be sure, Jacks were as plentiful as blackberries.

"And where may you be going?" asked the strange little old man. Jack wondered again – he was always wondering, you know – what the strange little old man had to do with it, but being always polite, he replied, "I am going to market to sell Milky-White and I mean to make a good bargain."

"So you will! So you will!" chuckled the strange little old man. "You look the sort of chap for it. I bet you know how many beans make five?"

"Two in each hand and one in my mouth," answered Jack readily. He really was sharp as a needle.

"Just so, just so!" chuckled the strange little old man, and as he spoke he drew out of his pocket five beans. "Well, here they are, so give us Milky-White."

Jack was so flabbergasted that he stood with his mouth open as if he expected the fifth bean to fly into it.

"What!" he said at last. "My Milky-White for five common beans! Not if I know it!"

"But they aren't common beans," put in the strange little old man, and there was a strange little smile on his strange little face. "If you plant these beans overnight, by morning they will have grown up right into the very sky."

Jack was too flabbergasted this time even to open his mouth; his eyes opened instead.

"Did you say right into the very sky?" he asked at last for, you see, Jack had wondered more about the sky than about anything else.

"Right up into the very sky," repeated the strange little old man, with a nod between each word. "It's a good bargain Jack and, as fair play's a jewel, if they don't, meet me here tomorrow morning and you shall have Milky-White back again. Will that please you?"

"Right as a trivet," cried Jack, without stopping to think, and the next moment he found himself standing on an empty road.

"Two in each hand and one in my mouth," repeated Jack. "That is what I said, and what I'll do. Everything in order, and if what the strange little old man said isn't true, I shall get Milky-White back tomorrow morning."

So whistling and munching the bean, he trudged home cheerfully, wondering what the sky would be like if he ever got there.

"What a long time you've been!" exclaimed his mother, who was watching anxiously for him at the gate. "It is past sun-setting, but I see you have sold Milky-White. Tell me quick how much you got for her."

"You'll never guess," began Jack.

"Laws-a-mercy! You don't say so," interrupted the good woman. "I've been worrying all day lest they should take you in. What was it? Ten pounds – fifteen – sure it *can't* be twenty!"

Jack held out the beans triumphantly.

"There," he said. "That's what I got for her, and a jolly good bargain too!"

It was his mother's turn to be flabbergasted, but all she said was, "What! Them beans!"

"Yes," replied Jack, beginning to doubt his own wisdom, "but they're magic beans. If you plant them overnight, by morning they - grow - right - up - into - the - sky - Oh! Please don't hit so hard!"

Jack's mother for once had lost her temper, and was belabouring the boy for all she was worth, and when she had finished scolding and beating, she flung the miserable beans out of the window and sent him, supperless, to bed.

If this was the magical effect of the beans, thought Jack ruefully, he didn't want any more magic, if you please. However, being healthy and as a rule, happy, he soon fell asleep and slept like a top.

When he woke he thought at first it was moonlight, for everything in the room showed greenish. Then he stared at the little window. It was covered as if with a curtain of leaves. He was out of bed in a trice, and the next moment, without waiting to dress, was climbing up the biggest beanstalk you ever saw. What the strange little old man had said was true! One of the beans which his mother had chucked into the garden had found soil, taken root, and grown in the night…

Where?... Up to the very sky? Jack meant to see at any rate.

So he climbed, and he climbed, and he climbed. It was easy work, for the big beanstalk with the leaves growing out of each side was like a ladder. He was soon out of breath, then got his second wind, and was just beginning to wonder if he had a third when he saw in front of him a wide, shining white road stretching away, and away, and away.

So he took to walking, and he walked, and walked, and walked, till he came to a tall shining white house with a wide white doorstep, and on the doorstep stood a great big woman with a black porridge-pot in her hand.

Now Jack, having had no supper, was hungry as a hunter, and when he saw the porridge-pot he said quite politely, "Good morning ma'm, I wonder if you could give me some breakfast?"

"Breakfast!" echoed the woman, who, in truth, was an ogre's wife. "If it is breakfast you're wanting, it's breakfast you'll likely be, for I expect my man home any instant and there is nothing he likes better for breakfast than a boy – a fat boy grilled on toast."

Now Jack was not a bit of a coward, and when he wanted a thing he generally got it, so he said cheerful-like, "I'd be fatter if I'd had my breakfast!" where at the ogre's wife laughed and bade Jack come in, for she was not really half as bad as she looked. Jack had hardly finished the great bowl of porridge and milk she gave him when the whole house began to tremble and quake. It was the ogre coming home!

Thump! THUMP!! THUMP!!!

"Into the oven with you, sharp!" cried the ogre's wife, and the iron oven door was just closed when the ogre strode in. Jack could see him through the little peephole slide at the top where the steam came out. He was a big one for sure. He had three sheep strung to his belt, and these he threw down on the table.

"Here, wife," he cried, "roast me these snippets for breakfast; they are all I've been able to get this morning, worse luck! I hope the oven's hot?" And he went to touch the handle, while Jack burst out all of a sweat wondering what would happen next.

"Roast?" echoed the ogre's wife. "Pooh! The little things would dry to cinders. Better boil them." So she set to work to boil them; but the ogre began sniffing about the room.

"They don't smell – mutton meat," he growled. Then he frowned horribly and began the real ogre's rhyme:

"Fee-fi-fo-fum,
I smell the blood of an Englishman.
Be he alive, or be he dead,
I'll grind his bones to make my bread."

"Don't be silly!" said his wife. "It's the bones of the little boy you had for supper that I'm boiling down for soup! Come, eat your breakfast, there's a good ogre!"

So the ogre ate his three sheep, and when he had done, he went to a big oaken chest and took out three big bags of golden pieces. These he put on the table, and began to count their contents while his wife cleared away the breakfast things. By and by his head began to nod, and at last he began to snore, and snored so loud that the whole house shook.

Then Jack nipped out of the oven and seizing one of the bags of gold, crept away, and ran along the straight, wide, shining white road as fast as his legs would carry him till he came to the beanstalk. He couldn't climb down it with the bag of gold as it was so heavy, so he just flung his burden down first and helter-skelter-like, climbed after it.

When he came to the bottom there was his mother picking up gold pieces out of the garden as fast as she could, for, of course, the bag had burst.

"Laws-a-mercy me!" she says. "Wherever have you been? See! It's been rainin' gold!"

"No, it hasn't," began Jack. "I climbed up..." Then he turned to look for the beanstalk, but lo and behold! It wasn't there at all. So he knew, then, it was all real magic.

After that they lived happily on the gold pieces for a long time and the

bedridden father got all sorts of nice things to eat, but at last a day came when Jack's mother showed a doleful face as she put a big yellow sovereign into Jack's hand and bade him be careful at the market, because there was not one more in the coffer. After that they must starve.

That night Jack went supperless to bed of his own accord. If he couldn't make money, he thought, at any rate he could eat less money. It was a shame for a big boy to stuff himself and bring no grist to the mill. He slept like a top, as boys do when they don't over eat themselves, and when he woke… Hey, presto! The whole room showed greenish, and there was a curtain of leaves over the window! Another bean had grown in the night, and Jack was up it like a lamplighter before you could say knife.

This time he didn't take nearly so long climbing until he reached the straight, wide, shining white road, and in a trice he found himself before the tall white house, whereon the wide white steps the ogre's wife was standing with the black porridge-pot in her hand. This time Jack was as bold as brass.

"Good morning ma'm" he said. "I've come to ask you for breakfast, for I had no supper, and I'm as hungry as a hunter."

"Go away, bad boy!" replied the ogre's wife. "Last time I gave a boy breakfast my man missed a whole bag of gold. I believe you are the same boy."

"Maybe I am, maybe I'm not," said Jack, with a laugh. "I'll tell you true when I've had my breakfast but not till then." So the ogre's wife, who was dreadfully curious, gave him a big bowl full of porridge, but before he had half finished it he heard the ogre coming –

Thump! THUMP!! THUMP!!!

"Into the oven with you," shrieked the ogre's wife. "You shall tell me when he has gone to sleep." This time Jack saw through the steam peephole that the ogre had three fat calves strung to his belt.

"Better luck today, wife!" he cried, and his voice shook the house. "Quick! Roast these trifles for my breakfast! I hope the oven's hot?" And he went to feel the handle of the door, but his wife cried out sharply, "Roast? Why, you'd have to wait hours before they were done! I'll grill them – see how bright the fire is!"

"Umph!" growled the ogre, and then he began sniffing and calling out:

"Fee-fi-fo-fum,
I smell the blood of an Englishman.
Be he alive, or be he dead,
I'll grind his bones to make my bread."

"Twaddle!" said the ogre's wife. "It's only the bones of the boy you had last week that I've put into the pig-bucket!"

"Umph!" said the ogre harshly, but he ate the grilled calves and then said to his wife, "Bring me my hen that lays the magic eggs. I want to see gold."

So the ogre's wife brought him a great, big, black hen with a shiny red comb. She plumped it down on the table and took away the breakfast things. Then the ogre said to the hen, "Lay!" and it promptly laid – what do you think? – a beautiful, shiny, yellow, golden egg!

"None so dusty, henny-penny," laughed the ogre. "I shan't have to beg as long as I've got you."

Then he said, "Lay!" once more, and lo and behold! There was another beautiful, shiny, yellow, golden egg!

Jack could hardly believe his eyes, and made up his mind that he would have that hen, come what might. So, when the ogre began to doze, he jumped out like a flash from the oven, seized the hen, and ran for his life! But, you see, hens always cackle when they leave their nests after laying an egg, and this one set up such a scrawing that it awoke the ogre.

"Where's my hen?" he shouted, and his wife came rushing in. They both rushed to the door, but Jack had got the better of them by a good start. All they could see was a little figure right away down the wide white road, holding a big, scrawing, cackling, fluttering, black hen by the legs!

How Jack got down the beanstalk he never knew. It was all wings, and leaves, and feathers, and cackling, but get down he did, and there was his mother wondering if the sky was going to fall!

The very moment Jack touched ground he called out, "Lay!" and the black hen ceased cackling and laid a great, big, shiny, yellow, golden egg. So everyone was satisfied and from that moment everybody had everything that money could buy. For, whenever they wanted anything, they just said, "Lay!" and the black hen provided them with gold.

But Jack began to wonder if he couldn't find something else besides money in the sky. So one fine, moonlit, midsummer night he refused his supper and before he went to bed, stole out to the garden with a big watering can and watered the ground under his window, for, thought he, "there must be two more beans somewhere, and perhaps it is too dry for them to grow." Then he slept like a top.

And lo and behold! When he awoke, there was the green light shimmering through his room, and there he was in an instant on the beanstalk, climbing, climbing, climbing for all he was worth, but this time he knew better than to ask for his breakfast, for the ogre's wife would be sure to recognise him, so he just hid in some bushes beside the great white house, till he saw her in the scullery. He then slipped in and hid himself in the copper, for he knew she would be sure to look in the oven first thing. By and by he heard –

Thump! THUMP!! THUMP!!!

Peeping through a crack in the copper-lid, Jack could see the ogre stalk in with three huge oxen strung at his belt, but this time, no sooner had the ogre got into the house than he begun shouting:

"Fee-fi-fo-fum,
I smell the blood of an Englishman.
But he alive, or be dead,
I'll grind his bones to make my bread."

For, you see, the copper-lid didn't fit tight like the oven door, and ogres have noses like a dog's for scent.

"Well, I declare, so do I!" exclaimed the ogre's wife. "It will be that horrid boy who stole the bag of gold and the hen. If so, he's hid in the oven!" But when she opened the door, lo and behold, Jack wasn't there! Only some joints of meat roasting and sizzling away.

Then she laughed and said, "You and me be fools for sure. Why, it's the boy you caught last night that I am getting ready for your breakfast. Yes, we be fools to take dead meat for live flesh! So eat your breakfast, there's a good ogre!" But the ogre, though he enjoyed roast boy very much, wasn't satisfied, and every now and then he would burst out with "Fee-fi-fo-fum," and get up and search the cupboards, keeping Jack in a fever of fear lest he should think of the copper. But he didn't, and when he had finished his breakfast he called out to his wife, "Bring me my magic harp! I want to be amused."

So she brought out a little harp and put it on the table, and the ogre leant back in his chair and said lazily: "Sing!"

And lo and behold! The harp began to sing. If you want to know what it sang about, why, it sang about everything! It sang so beautifully that Jack forgot to be frightened, and the ogre forgot to think of "Fee-fi-fo-fum," and fell asleep and did not snore.

Then Jack stole out of the copper like a mouse and crept hands and knees to the table, raised himself up ever so softly and laid hold of the magic harp, for he was determined to have it, but, no sooner had he touched it, than it cried out quite loud, "Master! Master!" so the ogre woke, saw Jack making off, and rushed after him.

My goodness, it was a race! Jack was nimble, but the ogre's stride was twice as long. So, though Jack turned, and twisted, and doubled like a hare, yet at last, when he got to the beanstalk, the ogre was not a dozen yards behind him. There wasn't time to think, so Jack just flung himself on to the stalk and began to go down as fast as he could while the harp kept calling, "Master! Master!" at the very top of its voice.

He had only got down about a quarter of the way when there was the most awful lurch you can think of and Jack nearly fell off the beanstalk. It was the ogre beginning to climb down, and his weight made the stalk sway like a tree in a storm. Jack knew it was life or death, and he climbed down faster and faster, and as he climbed he shouted, "Mother! Mother! Bring an axe! Bring an axe!"

Now his mother, as luck would have it, was in the back yard chopping wood, and she ran out thinking that this time the sky must have fallen. Just at the moment Jack touched the ground, he flung down the harp – which immediately began to sing of beautiful things – and seized the axe and gave a great chop at the beanstalk, which shook and swayed and bent like barley before a breeze.

"Have a care!" shouted the ogre, clinging on as hard as he could, but Jack did have a care, and he dealt that beanstalk such a shrewd blow that the whole of it, ogre and all, came toppling down and, of course, the ogre broke his crown so that he died on the spot.

After that everyone was quite happy, for they had gold and to spare, and if the bedridden father was sad, Jack just brought out the harp and said, "Sing!" and lo and behold, it sang about everything under the sun!

So Jack ceased wondering so much and became quite a useful person, and the last bean hasn't grown yet; it is still in the garden. I wonder if it will ever grow; and what little child will climb its beanstalk into the sky; and what will that child find? Goody me!

TRACK 25

Monday's Child Is Fair Of Face
Anon

Monday's child is fair of face,
Tuesday's child is full of grace,
Wednesday's child is full of woe,
Thursday's child has far to go,
Friday's child is loving and giving,
Saturday's child works hard for a living,
But the child that is born on the Sabbath day
Is bonny, and blithe, and good, and gay.

Frère Jacques

Traditional

Moderately

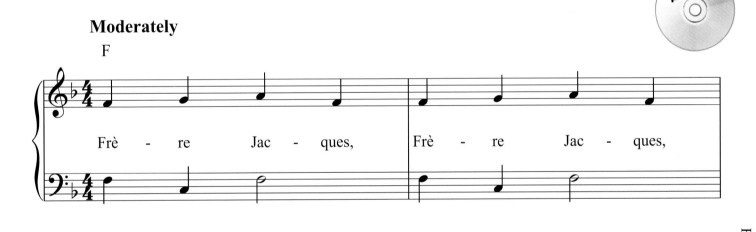

Frè - re   Jac - ques,   Frè - re   Jac - ques,

dor - mez vous?   Dor - mez vous?   Son - nez les ma - ti - nes,

son-nez les ma-ti-nes,   din don din!   Din don din!

Frère Jacques

Pat-*A*-Cake

Traditional

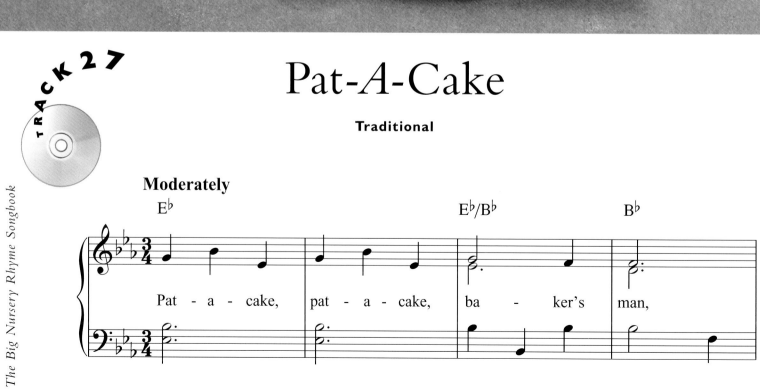

Pat - a - cake, pat - a - cake, ba - ker's man,

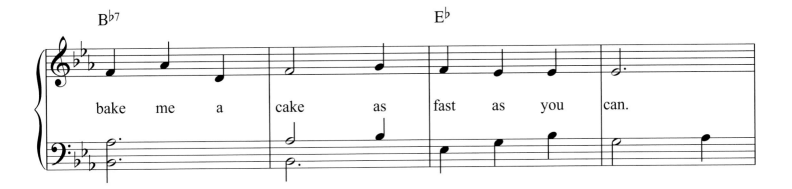

bake me a cake as fast as you can.

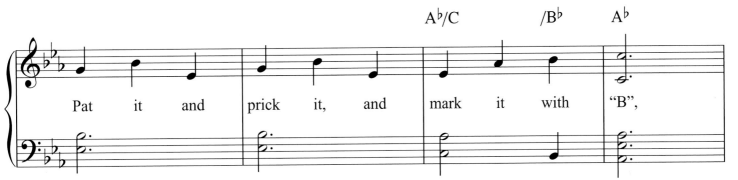

Pat it and prick it, and mark it with "B",

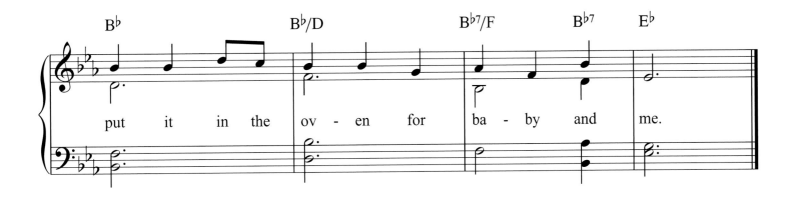

put it in the ov - en for ba - by and me.

Peter *Piper*

Traditional

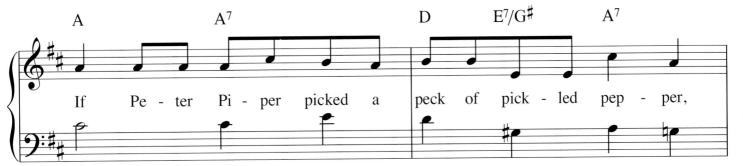

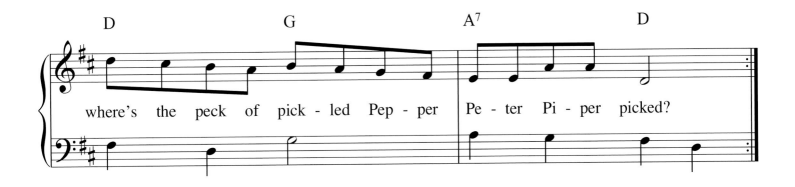

Polly *Put* The *Kettle* On

Traditional

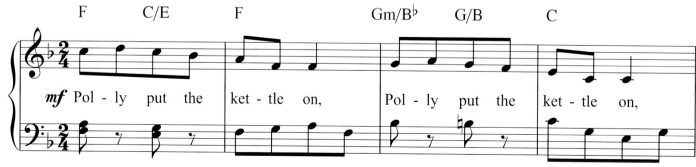

Moderately

Pol - ly put the ket - tle on, Pol - ly put the ket - tle on,

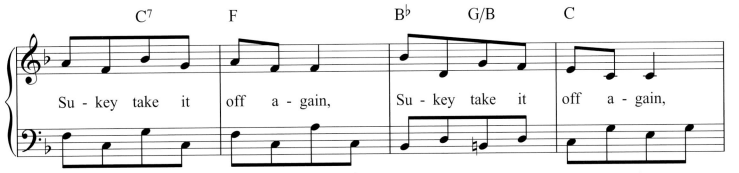

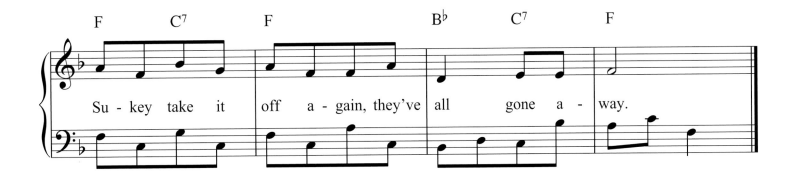

Pop Goes The Weasel

Traditional

Moderately

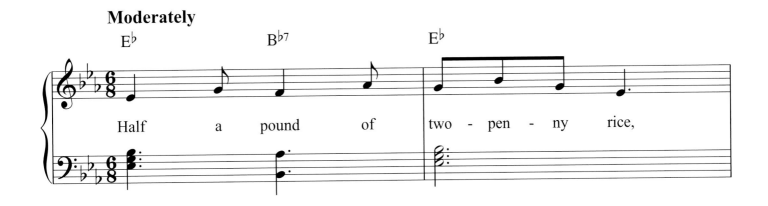

Half a pound of two - pen - ny rice,

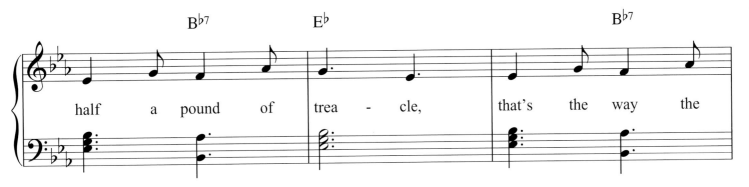

half a pound of trea - cle, that's the way the

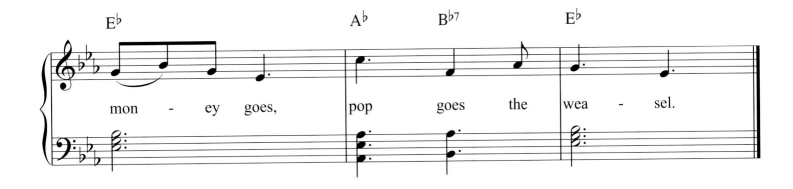

mon - ey goes, pop goes the wea - sel.

Ring-*A*-Ring O'Roses

Traditional

Moderately

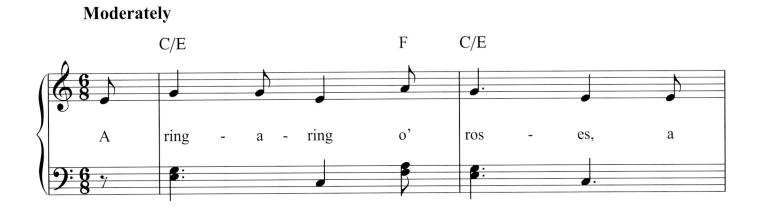

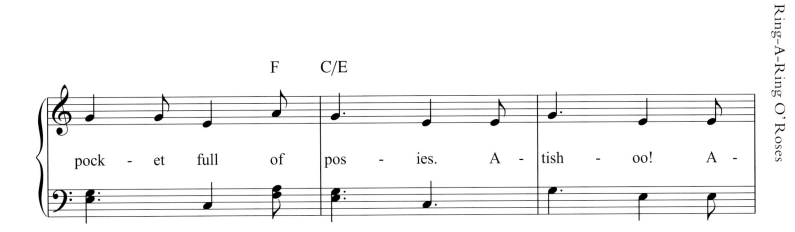

A ring - a - ring o' ros - es, a pock - et full of pos - ies. A - tish - oo! A - tish - oo! We all fall down._____

TRACK 32

Old *MacDonald*

Traditional

Bright

1. Old Mac - Don - ald had a farm, ee - eye, ee - eye,
(Verses 2-5 see block lyric)

oh!   And   on   that   farm   he   had   some   chicks,

Repeat as necessary

ee - eye,   ee - eye,   oh!   With   a   chick - chick   here,   and   a

chick chick there,   here a chick, there a chick,   ev - 'ry where a chick chick.

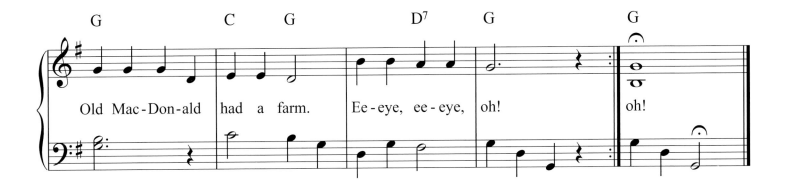

Old Mac-Don-ald   had   a   farm.   Ee - eye,   ee - eye,   oh!   oh!

Old MacDonald had a farm,
Ee-eye, ee-eye, oh!
And on that farm he had some ducks,
Ee-eye, ee-eye, oh!

2 With a quack-quack here and a quack-quack there,
Here a quack, there a quack, everywhere a quack-quack.
Chick-chick here and a chick-chick there,
Here a chick, there a chick, everywhere a chick-chick.
Old MacDonald had a farm,
Ee-eye, ee-eye, oh!

…and on that farm he had some cows…
With a moo-moo here and a moo-moo there,
3 Here a moo, there a moo, everywhere a moo-moo,
Quack-quack here and a quack-quack there…
Chick-chick here and a chick-chick there…

…and on that farm he had some pigs…
With an oink-oink here and an oink-oink there,
4 Here an oink, there an oink, everywhere an oink-oink,
Moo-moo here…
Quack-quack here…
Chick-chick here…

...and on that farm he had some sheep...
With a baa-baa here and a baa-baa there,
Here a baa, there a baa, everywhere a baa-baa,
5 Oink-oink here...
Moo-moo here...
Quack-quack here...
Chick-chick here...

Little *Red* Riding *Hood*
by *Charles* Perrault

Once upon a time there was a little girl who was called Little Red Riding Hood because she was quite small, and because she always wore a red cloak with a big red hood to it which her grandmother had made for her.

One day her mother, who had been churning and baking cakes, said to her, "My dear, put on your red cloak with the hood to it and take this cake and this pot of butter to your Grannie, and ask how she is, for I hear she is ailing."

Now Little Red Riding Hood was very fond of her grandmother who made her so many nice things, so she put on her cloak joyfully and started on her errand. But her grandmother lived some way off, and to reach the cottage Little Red Riding Hood had to pass through a vast lonely forest. However, some woodcutters were at work in it, so Little Red Riding Hood wasn't alarmed when she saw a great big wolf coming towards her, because she knew that wolves were cowardly things, and sure enough the wolf, though but for the woodcutters would surely have eaten Little Red Riding Hood, only stopped and asked her politely where she was going.

"I am going to see Grannie, take her this cake and this pot of butter, and ask how she is," says Little Red Riding Hood.

"Does she live a very long way off?" asks the wolf craftily.

"Not so very far if you go by the straight road," replied Little Red Riding Hood. "You only have to pass the mill and the first cottage on the right is Grannie's, but I am going by the wood path because there are such a lot of nuts and flowers and butterflies."

"I wish you good luck," says the wolf politely. "Give my respects to your grandmother and tell her I hope she is quite well." And with that he trotted off, but instead of continuing on his way, he turned back, took the straight road to the old woman's cottage, and knocked at the door.

Rap! Rap! Rap!

"Who's there?" asked the old woman, who was in bed.

"Little Red Riding Hood," sings out the wolf, making his voice as shrill as he could. "I've come to bring dear Grannie a pot of butter and a cake from Mother, and to ask how you are."

"Pull the bobbin and the latch will go up," says the old woman, well satisfied.

So the wolf pulled the bobbin, the latch went up, and oh my! It wasn't a minute before he had gobbled up old Grannie, for he'd had nothing to eat for a week.

Then he shut the door, put on Grannie's nightcap, got into bed and rolled himself well up in the clothes.

By and by along comes Little Red Riding Hood, who had been amusing herself by gathering nuts, running after butterflies, and picking flowers. She knocked at the door.

Rap! Rap! Rap!

"Who's there?" says the wolf, making his voice as soft as he could.

Now Little Red Riding Hood heard the voice was very gruff, but she thought her grandmother had a cold, so she said, "Little Red Riding Hood with a pot of butter and a cake from Mother to ask how you are."

"Pull the bobbin and the latch will go up."

So Little Red Riding Hood pulled the bobbin, the latch went up, and there, she thought, was her grandmother in the bed, for the cottage was so dark one could not see well. Besides, the crafty wolf turned his face to the wall at first, and he made his voice as soft as he could, when he said, "Come and kiss me, my dear."

Then Little Red Riding Hood took off her cloak and went to the bed.

"Oh, Grandmamma, Grandmamma," says she, "what big arms you've got!"

"All the better to hug you with," says he.

"But Grandmamma, Grandmamma, what big legs you have!"

"All the better to run with, my dear."

"Oh, Grandmamma, Grandmamma, what big ears you've got!"

"All the better to hear with, my dear."

"But Grandmamma, Grandmamma, what big eyes you've got!"

"All the better to see you with, my dear!"

"Oh, Grandmamma, Grandmamma, what big teeth you've got!"

"All the better to eat you with, my dear!" says that wicked, wicked wolf, and with that he gobbled up Little Red Riding Hood.

Sing A Song Of Sixpence

Traditional

Moderately bright

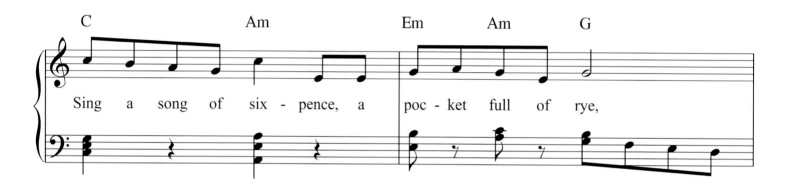

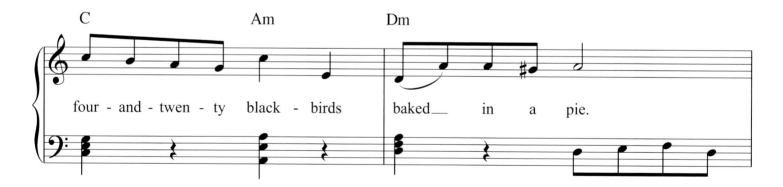

Sing a song of six - pence, a poc - ket full of rye,

four - and - twen - ty black - birds baked__ in a pie.

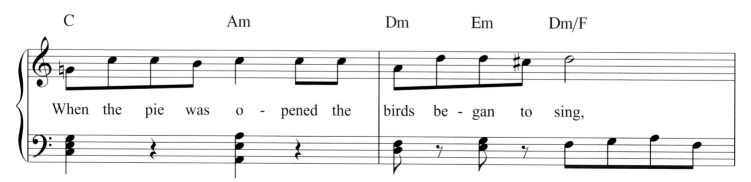

When the pie was o - pened the birds be - gan to sing,

The Big Nursery Rhyme Songbook

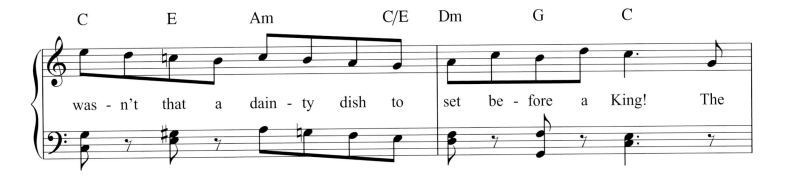

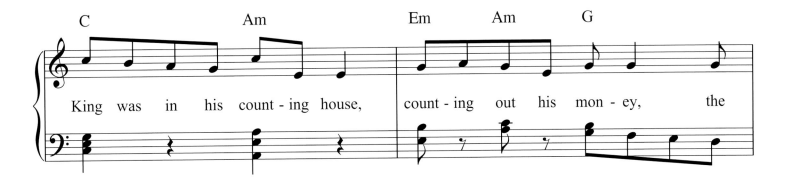

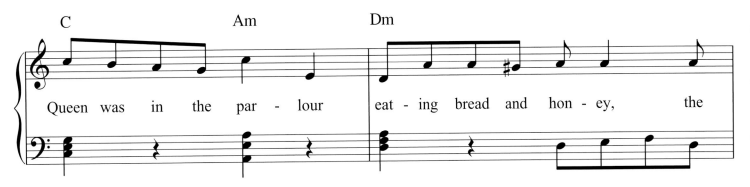

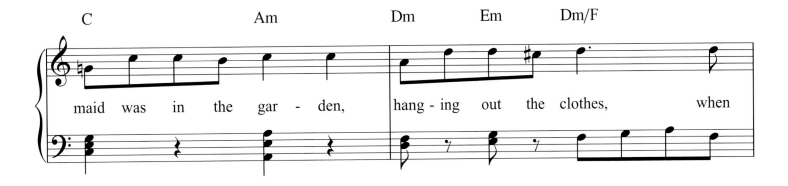

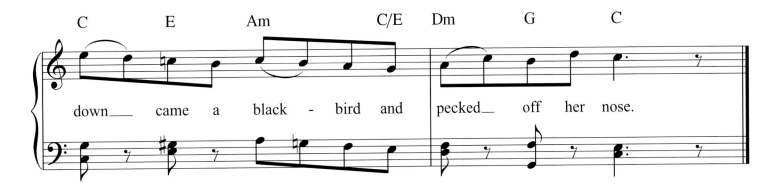

Row, *Row,* Row *Your* Boat

Traditional

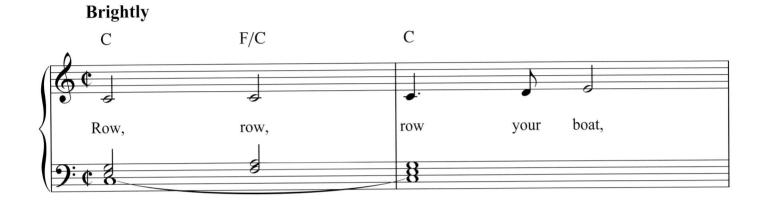

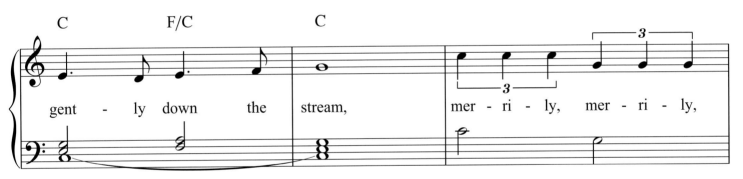

The *Muffin* Man

Traditional

TRACK 36

Moderately

| G | C/G | G | | Asus⁴ | A⁷ | | D |

Do you know the Muf - fin Man, the Muf - fin Man, the Muf - fin Man? Oh,

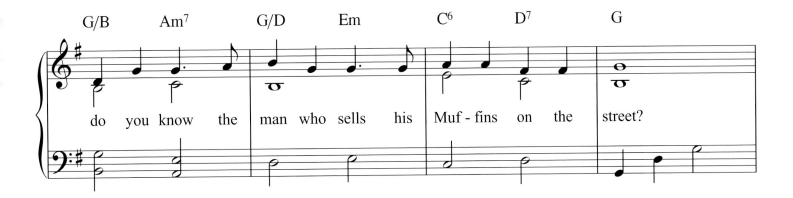

do you know the man who sells his Muf - fins on the street?

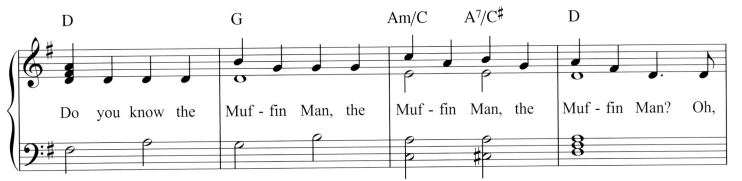

Do you know the Muf - fin Man, the Muf - fin Man, the Muf - fin Man? Oh,

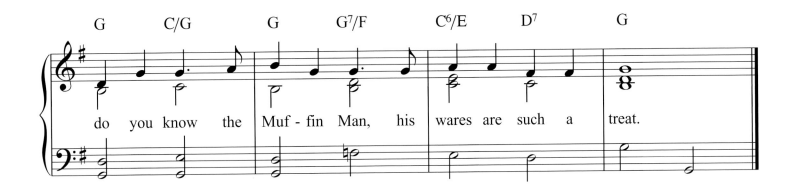

do you know the Muf - fin Man, his wares are such a treat.

TRACK 37

This *Old* Man, *He* Played *One*

Traditional

Moderately

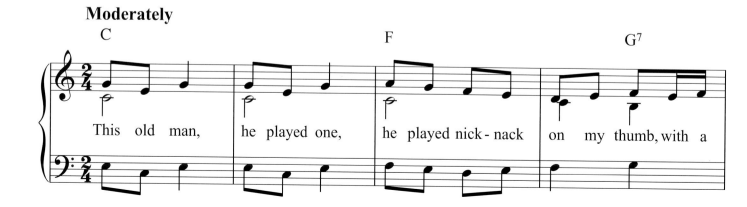

This old man, | he played one, | he played nick-nack | on my thumb, with a

The Big Nursery Rhyme Songbook

C   F   G   C G^7 C

nick - nack pad -dy whack give a dog a bone, this old man came roll - ing home.

2 This old man, he played two,
He played nick-nack on my shoe…

3 This old man, he played three…knee…

4 This old man, he played four…door…

5 This old man, he played five…hive…

6 This old man, he played six…sticks…

7 This old man, he played seven…up in heaven…

8 This old man, he played eight…gate…

9 This old man, he played nine…spine…

10 This old man, he played ten…once again…

TRACK **38**

Three *Blind* Mice

Traditional

Brightly

C	G⁷	C		
Three	blind	mice,_____	_____	three

blind mice.

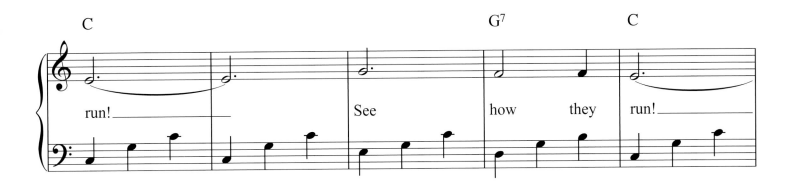

run! See how they run!

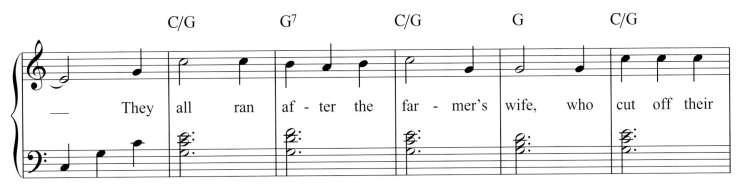

They all ran af - ter the far - mer's wife, who cut off their

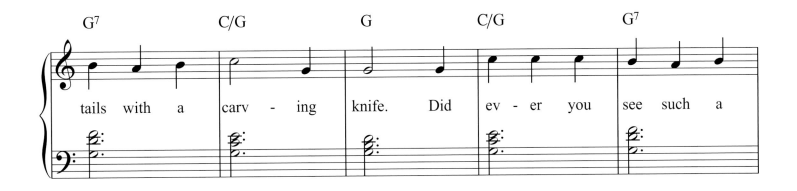

tails with a carv - ing knife. Did ev - er you see such a

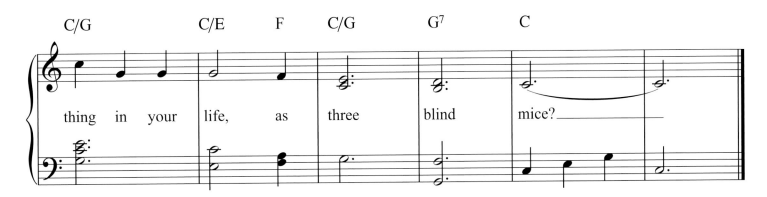

thing in your life, as three blind mice?

TRACK 39

Twinkle, *Twinkle* Little *Star*

Traditional

Sweetly

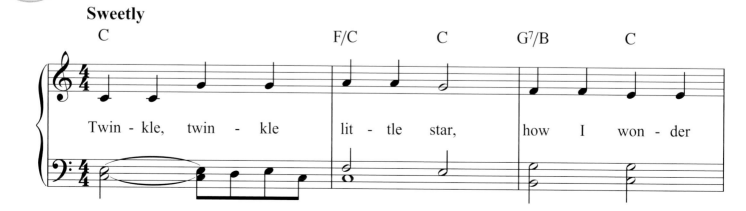

Twin - kle, twin - kle   lit - tle star,   how I won - der

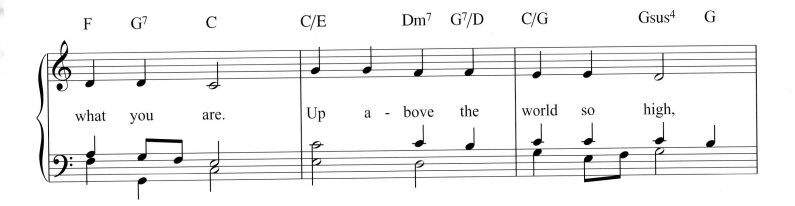

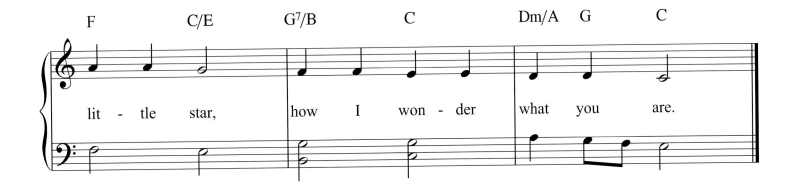

See-*Saw*, Margery *Daw*

Traditional

Smoothly

See - saw, Mar - ger - y Daw, Jack - y shall have a new mas - ter.

He shall have but a pen - ny a day, be - cause he can't work an - y fast - er.

The *Three* Little *Pigs*

Traditional

Once upon a time there was an old sow who had three little pigs, and as she had not enough for them to eat, she said they had better go out into the world and seek their fortunes.

Now, the eldest pig went first, and as he trotted along the road he met a man carrying a bundle of straw, so he said very politely, "If you please, sir, could you give me that straw to build me a house?"

The man, seeing what good manners the little pig had, gave him the straw and the little pig set to work and built a beautiful house with it.

Now, when it was finished, a wolf happened to pass that way, and he saw the house and smelt the pig inside. So he knocked at the door and said, "Little pig! Little pig! Let me in! Let me in!" But the little pig saw the wolf's big paws through the keyhole, so he answered back, "No! No! No! by the hair of my chinny-chin-chin!"

Then the wolf showed his teeth and said, "Then I'll huff, and I'll puff, and I'll blow your house in." So he huffed and he puffed and he blew the house in. Then he ate up the little piggy and went on his way.

Now, the next piggy, when he started out on his way, met a man carrying a bundle of furze and being very polite, he said to him, "If you please, sir, could you give me that furze to build me a house?" And the man, seeing what good manners the little pig had, gave him the furze and the little pig set to work and built himself a beautiful house.

Now, it so happened that when the house was finished, the wolf happened to pass that way. He saw the house, and he smelt the pig inside, so he knocked at the door and said, "Little pig! Little pig! Let me in! Let me in!" But the little pig peeped through the keyhole and saw the wolf's great ears, so he answered back, "No! No! No! by the hair of my chinny-chin-chin!"

Then the wolf showed his teeth and said, "Then I'll huff, and I'll puff, and I'll blow your house in!" So he huffed and he puffed and he blew the house in.

Then he ate up little piggy and went on his way.

Now, the third little piggy, when he started out on his way, met a man carrying a load of bricks and being very polite, he said, "If you please, sir, could you give me those bricks to build me a house?" And the man, seeing that he had been well-brought-up, gave him the bricks, and the little pig set to work and built himself a beautiful house.

Once again it happened that when it was finished, the wolf chanced to come that way. He saw the house, and he smelt the pig inside, so he knocked at the door and said, "Little pig! Little pig! Let me in! Let me in!" But the little pig peeped through the keyhole and saw the wolf's great eyes, so he answered, "No! No! No! by the hair of my chinny-chin-chin!"

"Then I'll huff, and I'll puff, and I'll blow your house in!" says the wolf, showing his teeth.

Well! He huffed and he puffed; he puffed and he huffed; and he huffed, huffed and he puffed, puffed, but he could *not* blow the house down. At last he was so out of breath that he couldn't huff and puff any more. So he thought a bit, then he said, "Little pig! I know where there is ever such a nice field of turnips."

"Do you," says little piggy, "and where might that be?"

"I'll show you," says the wolf. "If you will be ready at six o'clock tomorrow morning, I will call round for you, and we can go together to Farmer Smith's field and get turnips for dinner."

"Thank you kindly," says the little piggy. "I will be ready at six o'clock sharp." But you see, the little pig was not one to be taken in with chaff, so he got up at five, trotted off to Farmer Smith's field, rooted up the turnips, and was home eating them for breakfast when the wolf clattered at the door and cried, "Little pig, little pig, aren't you ready?"

"Ready?" says the little piggy. "Why! What a sluggard you are! I've been to the field and come back again, and I'm having a nice pot full of turnips for breakfast." The wolf grew red with rage, but he was determined to eat little piggy so he said, as if he didn't care, "I'm glad you like them, but I know something better than turnips."

"Indeed," says little piggy, "and what may that be?"

"A nice apple tree down in Merry Gardens with the juiciest, sweetest apples on it! So if you will be ready at five o'clock tomorrow I will come round for you and we can get the apples together."

"Thank you kindly," says little piggy. "I will be ready at five o'clock sharp."

Now, the next morning he bustled up ever so early, at four o'clock, and started to get the apples, but you see, the wolf had been taken in once and wasn't going to be taken in again, so he also started at four o'clock. The little pig had just got his basket half full of apples when he saw the wolf coming down the road licking his lips.

"Hullo!" says the wolf. "Here already? You *are* an early bird! Are the apples nice?"

"Very nice," says little piggy. "I'll throw you down one to try." And he threw it so far away, that when the wolf had gone to pick it up, the little pig was able to jump down with his basket and run home.

Well, the wolf was fair angry, but he went the next day to the little piggy's house and called through the door, as mild as milk, "Little pig! Little pig! You are so clever, I should like to give you a fairing, so if you will come with me to the fair this afternoon you shall have one."

"Thank you kindly," says little piggy. "What time shall we start?"

"At three o'clock sharp," says the wolf, "so be sure to be ready."

"I'll be ready before three," sniggered the little piggy, and he was!

He started early in the morning, went to the fair, rode in a swing, bought himself a butter-churn as a fairing, enjoyed himself ever so much, and trotted away towards home long before three o'clock. However, just as he got to the top of the hill, what should he see but the wolf coming up it, all panting and red with rage!

Well, there was no place to hide but in the butter-churn, so he crept into it and was just pulling down the cover when the churn started to roll down the hill – bumpety, bumpety, bump!

Of course piggy, inside, began to squeal and when the wolf heard the noise and saw the butter-churn rolling down on top of him – bumpety, bumpety, bump – he was so frightened that he turned tail and ran away. The wolf, however, was still determined to get the little pig for his dinner, so he went the next day to the house and told the little pig how sorry he was not to have been able to keep his promise of going to the fair, because of an awful, dreadful, terrible thing that had rushed at him, making a fearsome noise.

"Dear me!" says the little piggy. "That must have been me! I hid inside the butter-churn when I saw you coming, and it started to roll! I am sorry I frightened you!"

This was too much. The wolf danced about with rage and swore he would come down the chimney and eat up the little pig for his supper, but while he was climbing on to the roof, the little pig made up a blazing fire and put on a big pot full of water to boil. Then, just as the wolf was coming down the chimney, the little piggy whipped off the lid, and plump, in fell the wolf into the scalding water.

So the little piggy put on the cover again, boiled the wolf up, and ate *him* for supper.

Go To Bed Early
Anon

Go to bed early – wake up with joy;

Go to bed late – cross girl or boy;

Go to bed early – ready for play;

Go to bed late – moping all day;

Go to bed early – no pains or ills;

Go to bed late – doctors and pills;

Go to bed early – grow very tall;

Go to bed late – stay very small.